# THE BIG BOOK OF
# KIDS' JOKES

## for Aiden, Archie, Elias & Jules

ISBN: 978-1726200745

Published by Silversphere Media

A wholly owned subsidiary of The Sovereign Media Group

# THE BIG BOOK OF DAD JOKES

Animal Antics.................................................1

All Out to Sea...............................................7

Flies, Bugs & Crawlies..................................13

Birds of a Feather.......................................17

Dog Gone....................................................20

General Silliness..........................................23

Letters & Numbers......................................29

Magic Ghosts & Ghouls...............................31

Hippos & Elephants.....................................37

School Daze.................................................45

Let's Eat.....................................................49

Udderly Fantastic........................................55

What do you call that?................................57

Wit & Wear.................................................59

Wild Weather..............................................61

The Cat's Meow..........................................65

Kock Knock................................................69

Kids Crossword PUZZLES.............................75

Colouring Quizes........................................84

Litter Box

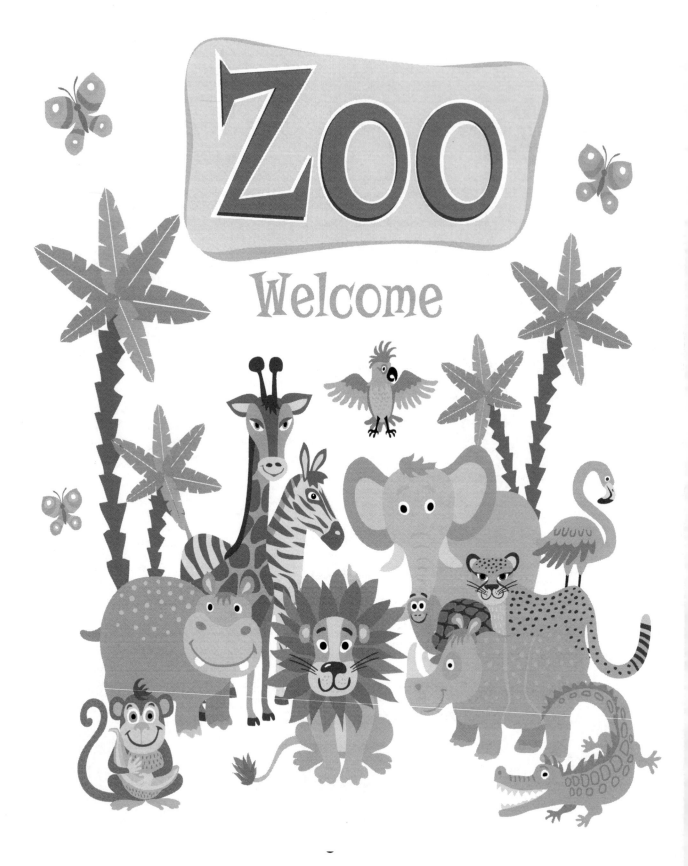

# ANIMAL ANTICS

Q. What do you call a bear
with no teeth?
A. A gummy bear.

Q. Why did the teddy take
off his shoes?
A. He preferred bear feet.

Q. What do you call bears with no ears?    A. B.

Q. What did the monkey
say when he got asked
for a date?
A. Sorry I only have
bananas.

Q. What does Mickey Mouse's wife drive?
Q. A Minnie van.

Q: What looks like half a donkey.
A: The other half of a donkey.

1

Q. Why didn't the dog want to play cards
with the cat?
A. He thought he was a cheetah.

Q. What do you call a deer with no eyes?
A. No eyed deer.

Q. Why do dragons sleep during the day?
A. So they can fight knights!

Q: What animal can jump higher
than a house?
A: Any animal. Houses can't jump.

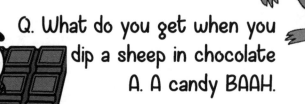

Q. What do you get when you
dip a sheep in chocolate
A. A candy BAAH.

Q. What do you call a cross between a
polar bear and a monkey?
A. A cross.

Q. Where do polar bears
cast their vote?
A. The North Poll.

Q. What do you call a blind dinosaur?
A. He-never-saw-us.

Q. Why can't you hear a Pterodactyl
go to the bathroom?
A. Because the PEE is silent.

Q. What do you call 50 rabbits
walking backwards?
A. A receding hare line.

Q. Where did the sheep get a hair cut?
A. At the baa-baa shop.

Q. How do you get a squirrel
to like you?
A. Just act like a nut!

Q. How did the lion say to the zebra?
A. Pleased to eat you!

Q. What kind of lion never roars?
A dandelion!

Q. What do you call a
flea infested rabbit?
A. Bugs Bunny.

Q. Why did the pony go to the doctor?
A. He was a little horse.

Q. Why do cowboys ride horses?
A. Because they are too heavy to carry.

Q. Where do horses like to live?
A. In neigh-borhoods.

Q. What kind of fly has a frog
in its throat?
A. A hoarse fly!

Q. What kind of shoes do frogs wear?
A. Open toad sandals.

Q. What has more lives than a cat?
A. A frog. A frog can croak every night!

Q. What do Winnie the Pooh and
Kermit the Frog have in common?
A. The same middle name.

Q. Why can't frogs tell stories?
A. Because they don't have tales.

Q. How did the frog fix his computer?
A. He ate all the bugs.

Q. What happened to the frog that parked illegally?
A. He got TOAD!!

4

Q. What do you call an alligator with a vest?
A. An investigator.

Q. What call an alligator without a vest?
A. Naked

Q. When does an alligator go meow?
A. When it's learning a new language.

Q. What do you call an alligator with a parsnip in each ear?
A. Anything you want, he can't hear you.

Q. What kind of key can't open any lock?
A. A mon-KEY.

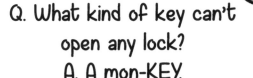

Q. How do you treat a pig with a grazed knee?
A. Clean it up and apply an Oinkment.

Q. When is it bad luck to see a black cat?
A. When you're a mouse.

# ALL OUT TO SEA

Q. What do you call a snail that is in the Navy?

A. A snailor!

Q. What lies at the bottom of the ocean and twitches uncontrollably?
A. A nervous wreck!

Q. What did the seaweed say when it got caught by a mussel?
A. Kelp, kelp!

Q. Why didn't the blind man eat fish?
A. He just couldn't sea-food.

Q. What kind of hair does the ocean have?
A. Wavy.

Q. What happened when the red ship smashed into the blue ship? A. All the sailors were marooned.

Q. What did one ocean say to the other ocean? A. Nothing, they just waved!

Q. What washes up on tiny beaches?
A. Microwaves.

Q. Why did the singer go sailing?

A. Because he wanted to hit the high C's.

Q. What did the pirate say on his 80th birthday?
A. Aye Matey.

Q. Why did the boy throw oranges into the ocean?
A. He wanted a Fanta-sea.

Q. How much does a pirate pay for earrings?
A. About a buck an ear (buccaneer).

Q. What did the pirate get on his school report?
A. Seven C's.

Q: What would you call Captain Jack
Sparrow with a cat on his shoulder?
A: A purr-ate!

Q. What's a pirate's favourite letter?
A: Arrrrrr!

Q.How do you split the sea in two?
A. Use a sea-saw.

Q. What did the sand say to the
wave when the tide came in?
A. Hey, long time no sea.

Q. Why didn't the fish get into Harvard?
A. Because he was always below C - level.

Q. Why are fish so smart?
A. Because they live in schools!

Q. Why do fish live in salt water?
A. Because pepper makes them sneeze!

Q. Why are fish so easy to weigh?
A. Because they always have scales.

Q: What did the octopus say to his girlfriend when he proposed?
A: Can I have your hand, hand, hand, hand, hand, hand, hand, hand in marriage?

Q. What kind of fish only swim at night?
A. A starfish!

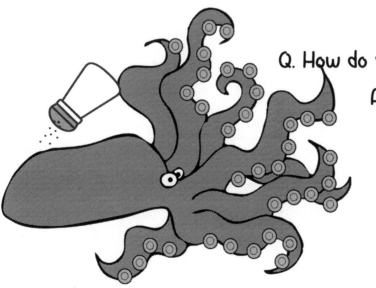

Q. How do you make an octopus laugh?
A. With Tentacles!

Q. What did one fish say to the other?
A. Keep your mouth shut and you'll never get caught.

9

Q. Why did the fish blush?
A. Because the sea weed.

Q. Why don't lobsters give to charity?
A. Because they're totally shellfish.

Q. Where do crabs keep their money?
A. In a sand banks.

Q: What are the strongest creatures in the ocean?
A: Mussels.

Q. Where do shellfish go to get a quick loan?
A. The prawn broker.

Q. Why do sharks eat raw fish?
A. Because you can't cook underwater.

Q. What do you call a shark with a migraine?
A. A hammer head.

Q. What is shark's favourite sandwich?
A. Peanut butter and Jellyfish.

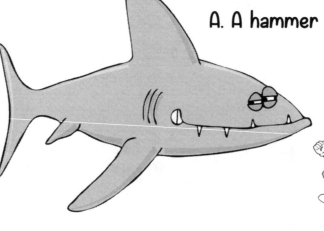

Q. Why did the detective investigate the tuna?
A. He thought it was behaviour was a bit fishy.

Q. Where do fish put their money?
A. In a river bank!

Q. Where can you find an ocean that has no water?
A. On a map!

Q. What is a knight's favourite fish?
A. A swordfish.

Q. Why was the dolphin so sad?
A. Because he had no PORPOISE in life!

12

# FLIES, BUGS, & CRAWLIES

Q: What goes 99 thump, 99 thump, 99 thump?
A: A centipede with a wooden leg.

Q: What is firmly on the ground and
a hundred feet in the air?
A: A centipede on its back!

Q. What do you get when you cross a
centipede with a parrot?
A. a walkie-talkie.

Q: Why was the butterfly thrown
out of the dance?
A: Because it was a moth ball

Q: Why wouldn't the fly use a computer?
A: He didn't want to get stuck on the world wide web.

Q. What do you call
a dead fly?
A. A flew.

Q. What do you call a
fly that can't fly?
A. A walk.

Q. What kind of fly goes well on toast?
A. A butter-fly

13

Q: What do you call two ants
that run away to get married?
A: Ant-elopes!

Q. How do you find a spider
in your computer?
A. Visit their website.

Q. What does a spider
wear to get married?
A. A webbing dress.

Q: When did the fly fly?
A: When the spider spied her!

Q. What did the ant stay inside the house?
A. He was a permanAnt resident.

Q: Who comes to a picnic but is never invited?
A: Ants.

Q: Why was the young ant confused?
A: Because all of his uncles were "ants".

Q: Why are flowers like A's?
A: Because bee's come after them!

Q. What do you call an American Bee?
A. A USB

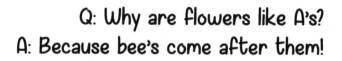

Q: What's smarter than a talking parrot?
A: A spelling bee!

14

# A CRAWLIE CROSSWORD

16

# BIRDS OF A FEATHER

Q: What type of key can't open a door?
A: A turkey!

Q: Why don't you take turkeys to church?
A: They use fowl language.

Q. What do you call two birds in love?
A. Tweethearts!

Q: Why don't ducks ever have spare change?
A: They only carry bills.

Q. Why did the early bird get up late?
A. Because he slept in.

Q: What is it called when a chicken fumbles with the ball?
A: A fowl play.

Q. Why did the duck refuse to pay his hospital bill?

A. ßHe thought the doctor was a quack.

Q. When is chicken soup bad for you?
A. When you are the chicken.

Q. What do you get when a pigeon
lays an egg on your roof?
A. An egg roll.

Q. What kind of bird is always sad?

A. A Blue jay.

Q. What kind of birds work
on construction sites?
A. Cranes!

Q. What did the turkey eat for dessert?

A. Peach gobbler.

Q. Why do birds lay eggs?

A. Because if they dropped them they would break.

Q: What do chickens like to do
on sunny days?
A: Go out for a peck-nic!

Q. Why was the dead
canary so expensive?
A. Because it never went
cheap.

Q Why did the chicken get arrested?
A. It was suspected of fowl play.

Q: Why can't you take a chicken to church?
A: They use fowl language.

Q. Why did the bird sit on the tomahawk
A. To hatchet.

Q What side of a chicken has
the most feathers?
A. The outside.

Q. What the most musical part
of a chicken?
A. The drumsticks.

19

# DOG GONe

Q. Why did the dog sleep under the car?
A. Because he wanted to wake up oily.

Q. Why can't Dalmatians hide?
A. Because they are always spotted.

Q. Where would you find a
dog with no legs?
A. Exactly where you left it!

Q. What do you call a dog with two broken legs?
A. It doesn't matter, it won't ever come!

Q. Where do dogs go when
they lose their tails?
A. They go to a retail store.

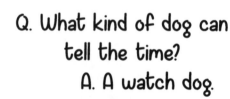

Q. What kind of dog can
tell the time?
A. A watch dog.

Q. Why can't people hear a dog whistle?
A. Because dogs can not whistle.

Q: What is a dog's favourite vegetable?
A: A collie-flower!

Q. What do you get if you cross
a dog with a telephone?
A. A golden receiver.

Q. When is a black dog not black?
A. When it's a greyhound.

Q. What is totally funny and
makes dogs itch?
A. The Flea Stooges!

Q. How did the dog
like his eggs?
A Pooched

Q: Why is a tree like a big dog?
A: They both have a lot of bark!

Q. Where did the dog do his shopping?
A. At the flea markets!

Q. Why was the dog thrown our
of the flea circus?
A. Because he stole the show.

Q. Why don't blind people go skydiving?
A. It scares the life out of their dogs.

21

# GENERAL SILLINESS

Q. What does a mirror look like really close up?

A. An eyeball.

Q. Did you hear about the expert sleeper?

A. She could do it with her eyes closed.

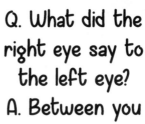

Q. What do you find inside a clean nose?

A. Fingerprints.

Q. What did the right eye say to the left eye?

A. Between you and me, something smells!

Q. What did the nose say to the finger?

A. Quit picking on me!

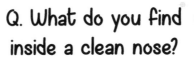

Q. How do you make a tissue dance?

A: You put a little boogie in it.

Q. What runs but never walks?

A. A tap.

Q. What runs faster, hot or cold?

A. Hot. Everyone can catch a cold.

Q. How much did the shop keeper charge for dead batteries?
A. Nothing, they were free of charge.

Q. What always gets answers but never asks anything?
A. A cell phone.

Q. What do you get when you drop a piano down a coal mine?
A. A flat minor

Q. What goes down but doesn't come up?
A. A yo.

Q. Why did the man want his spine removed?
A. He thought it was only holding him back

Q. Why couldn't the girl get into the library?
A. It was fully booked

Q. Why did the burglar take a shower?
A. He wanted to make a clean get away.

Q. Did you hear about the fire at the circus?
A. It was in tents!

Q. What do you call a rich elf?
A. Elfy.

Q. Why is it impossible to borrow money from a leprechaun?
A. Because he's always short.

Q. What did the boy do when his dentist told him to have a good day?
A. He went home.

Q. Why is Peter Pan always flying?
A. He Neverlands.

Q. What do call a smelly fairy?
A. Stinkerbell.

Q. Why did the hairdresser get to work early
A. She had a short cut

Q. Why did the girl pull her knees up to her chest and lean forward?
A. That's just how she rolls.

Q. What stays in the corner but travels the world?
A. A stamp.

Q. What do you call an electric daffodil?
A. A power plant.

Q. What did the big flower say to the little flower?
A. Hi, bud!

Q. What do you call a smart group of trees?
A. A brainforest.

Q. Why did the farmer bury his cash?
A. He wanted to make his soil rich!

Q. What is the world's mouthiest flower?
A. Two lips!

Q. What kind of tree fits in your hand?
A. A palm tree.

Q. What did the leaves name their sons?
A. Russell.

Q. Why did the scarecrow win an award?
A. Because he was outstanding in his field.

Q. Why did the girl tip toe past the medicine cabinet?
A. She didn't want to wake up the sleeping pills.

Q. How do you make a Venetian blind?
A. Poke him in the eye.

Q. Why was the astronomer always happy at sunset?
A. Because the rotation of the earth made his day.

Q. What's the difference between a tennis ball and the Prince of Wales?
A. One is heir to the throne and the other is thrown into the air.

Q. Why was the mushroom always throwing parties?
A. Because he was a fungi!

Q. What kind of bow doesn't use any arrows?
A. A bowtie.

Q. Did you hear about the woman who was scared of elevators?
A. She had to take steps to avoid them.

Q. Why are roofs so much smarter than walls?
A. Because they are always going over their heads.

Q. What is always running but never moves?
A. Your fridge.

Q. How do scientists freshen their breath?
A. With experi-mints!

Q. Why was the Japanese man broke?
A. He had Origami business, but it folded.

Q. If you are holding three watermelons and two eggs in your left hand, what would you have?
A. Really big hands!

# LETTERS & NUMBERS

Q. What starts with an E, ends with an E and only has one letter in it?
A. An Envelope

Q: What did 0 say to 8?
A: Nice belt!

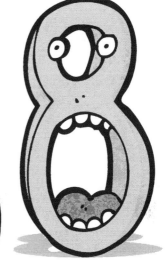

Q. What did the square say to the old circle?
A. Been around long?

Q. Why is 6 scared of 7?
A. Because 7 ate 9 and 10.

Q. Why did the nickel come second in the math quiz?
A. Because the dime had more cents.

Q. What has three feet but no legs?
A. A yard Stick.

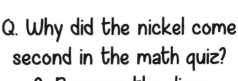 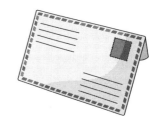

Q. What kind of plants are good at math?
A. Ones with square roots.

# MAGIC, GHOSTS & GHOULS

Q. Why did the fortune teller go out of business?
   A. She just didn't make a good prophet.

Q. Why did the psychic give up fortune telling?
A. She could see there was no future in it.

Q. What do you call a chubby psychic?
   A. A four-chin teller.

Q. What do ghosts like for dinner?
   A Spooketti.

Q. What do ghosts do
when it gets too hot?
A. They turn on the
scare conditioner.

Q. Why are all ghosts such terrible liars?
A. Because you always can see right
through them.

Q. Why did the ghost leave the disco?
A. He had no body to dance with.

31

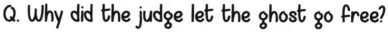

Q. What's it called when a ghost makes a mistake?
A. A boo boo!

Q. Why did the judge let the ghost go free?
A. They just couldn't pin anything on him.

Q. Why was the ghost a really good lawyer?
A. He always gave a spirited defence.

Q. Why do ghosts hate rainy days?
A. They dampen their spirits.

Q. Why did the ghost take the elevator?
A. He wanted to lift his spirits.

Q. Why didn't the other ghost take the elevator?
A. He preferred to use the scare-case.

Q. What do you eat at
a horror movie?
A. I scream.

Q: What is an owl's
favourite holiday?
A: Owl-oween!

Q. What do you call a really nice monster?
A. A total failure.

Q. How do you make a skeleton crack up?
A. Tickle his funny bone.

Q. Why are skeletons so cool and relaxed?
A. Because nothing gets under their skin.

Q. Why don't skeletons go skydiving?
A. They just don't have the guts.

Q. Why wouldn't the skeleton get a job?
A. He was a lazy bones.

Q. What do you call two witches
that share a house?
A. Broom-mates.

Q. Why do witches wear pointy hats?
A. To keep their heads warm.

Q. Why won't witches ride their
brooms when they are angry?
A. They are afraid they might fly off
the handle.

Q. What is a witch's
favourite subject?
A. Spelling!

Q. Why do witches wear nametags?
A. So you can tell which witch is which!

Q. Why don't mummies have any friends?
A. They are all wrapped up in themselves.

34

Q. Why did the vampire get thrown off the baseball team?
A. Because he was being a pain in the neck.

Q. Did you hear about the vampire that Q. loved baseball?
A: He turned into a bat.

Q. Where do vampires live?
A. On a dead end street.

Q. Where do vampire go to buy pencils?
A: Pencil-vania.

Q. Why did the vampire use mouthwash?
A. He had BAT breath.

Q. Why is it easy to trick a vampire?
A. Because they are total suckers.

Q. What do you get when you cross
a vampire with a teacher?
A. A blood test.

Q: What kind of dogs do vampires have?

A: Blood-hounds.

Q. What is a vampires favourite
fruit?
A. A NECK-tarine.

Q. Why didn't the vampire drink the coffee?
A. It was de-coffin-ated!

Q. What do you get when you cross a
snowman and a vampire?
A: Frostbite!

# HIPPOS & ELEPHANTS

Q: What do you get when you cross a fish with an elephant?

A: Swimming trunks.

Q. What's grey with red spots?

A. An elephant with the measles.

Q: Why do elephants never forget?

A: Because nobody tells them anything.

Q: What's the difference between an egg and an elephant?

A: If you don't know, I'm not asking you to get eggs.

Q. What did the banana say to the elephant?

A. Nothing. Bananas can't talk!

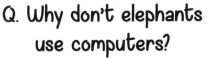

Q. Why don't elephants
use computers?
A. Because they're afraid
of the mouse.

Q. What's as big as an elephant, but
weighs nothing?
A: An elephant's shadow.

Q. How do you know if an elephant is standing
next to you in an elevator?
A. The strong smell of peanuts on their breath.

Q. What do elephants do to relax?
A. They Watch elevision.

Q. What do you call an elephant in a elevator?

A. Stuck.

Q. How do you stop an elephant from charging?
A. Take away their credit card.

Q. Why aren't elephants allowed in the Spa?
A. Because they can't keep their trunks up.

Q. What happens when elephants get lightheaded?
A. They ele-faint.

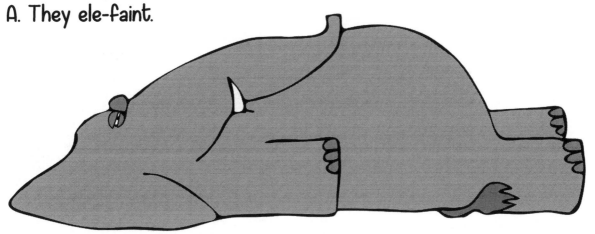

Q. Why did the elephant lie down in the middle of the road?
A. To stop the chicken from crossing.

Q: How do elephants get out of the bath?
A: Wet and wrinkled.

Q: What's weighs 2 tons,
has big ears and makes
toys for Santa?
A: Elfants!

Q: What time is it when an elephant sits on your fence?
A: Time to get a new fence.

Q: What game should you never play with an elephant?
A: Squash!

Q: What do you do with a green elephant?
A: Wait until it is ripe.

Q: What do you do with a blue elephant?
A: Tell it funny jokes.

Q: What is the biggest kind of ant?
A: An eleph-ant.

Q: What to elephants and trees have in common?
A: They both have trunks.

Q: Why wont they let elephants travel on planes?
A: They don't carry trunks in the passenger cabin.

Q: What do you give a seasick elephant?
A: A very big bag.

Q: How do elephants get down from a ladder?
A: They don't, they get their down from a goose.

Q: What do you call an elephant on a school bus?
A: A passenger.

Q: Why do girl elephants wear pink tutus?
A: So you can tell them from boy elephants.

41

Q. What do you call
an untidy hippo?
A. A hippoto-Mess.

Q. How do you get a hippo to
act like a chicken?
A. Hippo-notise him.

Q. What kind of music
do hippos like?
A. Hippo-Hop.

Q. What happens if
you leave a hippo out
in the snow?
A. They get hippo-
thermia.

.Q: Q. How do you
vaccinate a hippo?
A: With a
hippodermic needle.

Q. What is as big as
a hippo but weighs
nothing?
A. It's shadow.

Q. Why do you never see hippos hiding in trees?
A. Because they are really good at it.

42

FIND
ONE
OF A KIND

# SCHOOL
## Crossword Puzzle

STATIONERY

BOOK

UNIFORM

| B | C | O | O | K | L | A | P | T | O | P | H |
| O | O | W | A | T | E | R | B | O | T | T | L | E |
| O | O | S | T | A | T | I | O | N | E | R | Y |
| K | K | S | E | P | X | H | D | V | N | E | H | U | F |
| F | B | H | N | O | N | E | H | C | E | C | W |
| P | U | P | A | C | O | U | S | H | L | E | M |
| G | P | N | F | N | T | O | N | W | I | V | N |
| L | N | R | I | R | E | S | F | F | B | A | G |
| O | E | T | H | F | B | T | T | H | O | Z | N |
| B | O | E | H | O | O | B | C | A | M | I | D |
| E | U | G | N | D | O | R | E | C | W | U | X |
| F | B | G | F | C | K | X | M | S | H | P | J |

BAG

WATER BOTTLE

MOBILE

GLOBE

LAPTOP

NOTEBOOK

# SCHOOL DAZE!

Q. Did you hear about the cross eyed teacher?
A. She couldn't control his pupils.

Q. Why did the kid eat his homework?
A. Because his teacher said it was a
piece of cake!

Q. Why did the balloon skip school?
A. They were having a pop quiz.

Q. Did you hear about the kidnapping at school?
A. It turned out OK. He woke up.

Q. How do bees get to school?
A. On the school buzz, of course!

Q. What do elves
learn in school?
A. The elf-abet.

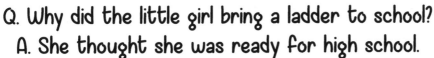

Q. Why did the little girl bring a ladder to school?
A. She thought she was ready for high school.

Q. Where do you go to learn how to make desserts?
A. Sundae school.

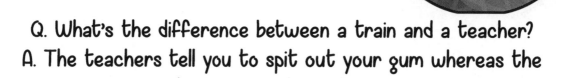

Q. What did the paper say to the pencil?
A. Write on!

Q. What's the difference between a train and a teacher?
A. The teachers tell you to spit out your gum whereas the train says "chew chew".

Q. Why was the magician such a good student?
A. He was good at trick questions.

Q. Why couldn't the cyclops teach team sports?
A. He only had one pupil.

Q. What kind of school did the surfer go to?
A. Boarding school.

Q: What happens when put a plant in math class?
A: It grows square roots.

Q. Where did Sir Lancelot go to school?
A. Knight school.

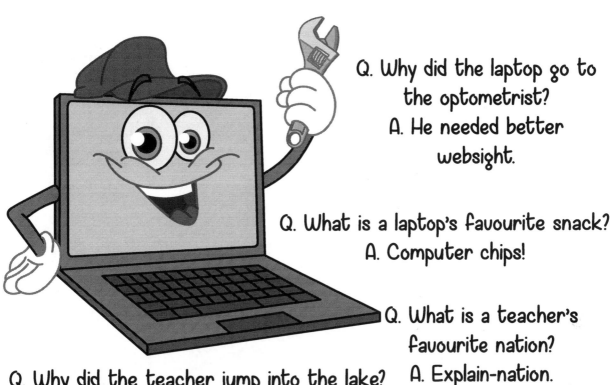

Q. Why did the laptop go to the optometrist?
A. He needed better websight.

Q. What is a laptop's favourite snack?
A. Computer chips!

Q. What is a teacher's favourite nation?
A. Explain-nation.

Q. Why did the teacher jump into the lake?
A. She wanted to test the waters.

Q. What happen to the boy who took the school bus home?
A. His dad made him bring it back!

Q. What do geometry teachers eat?
A. Square meals.

Q. Why did the teacher marry the Cleaner?
A. Because she swept him off his feet.

Q. Why don't you ever see a giraffe in elementary school?
A. Because they all go to HIGH School!

47

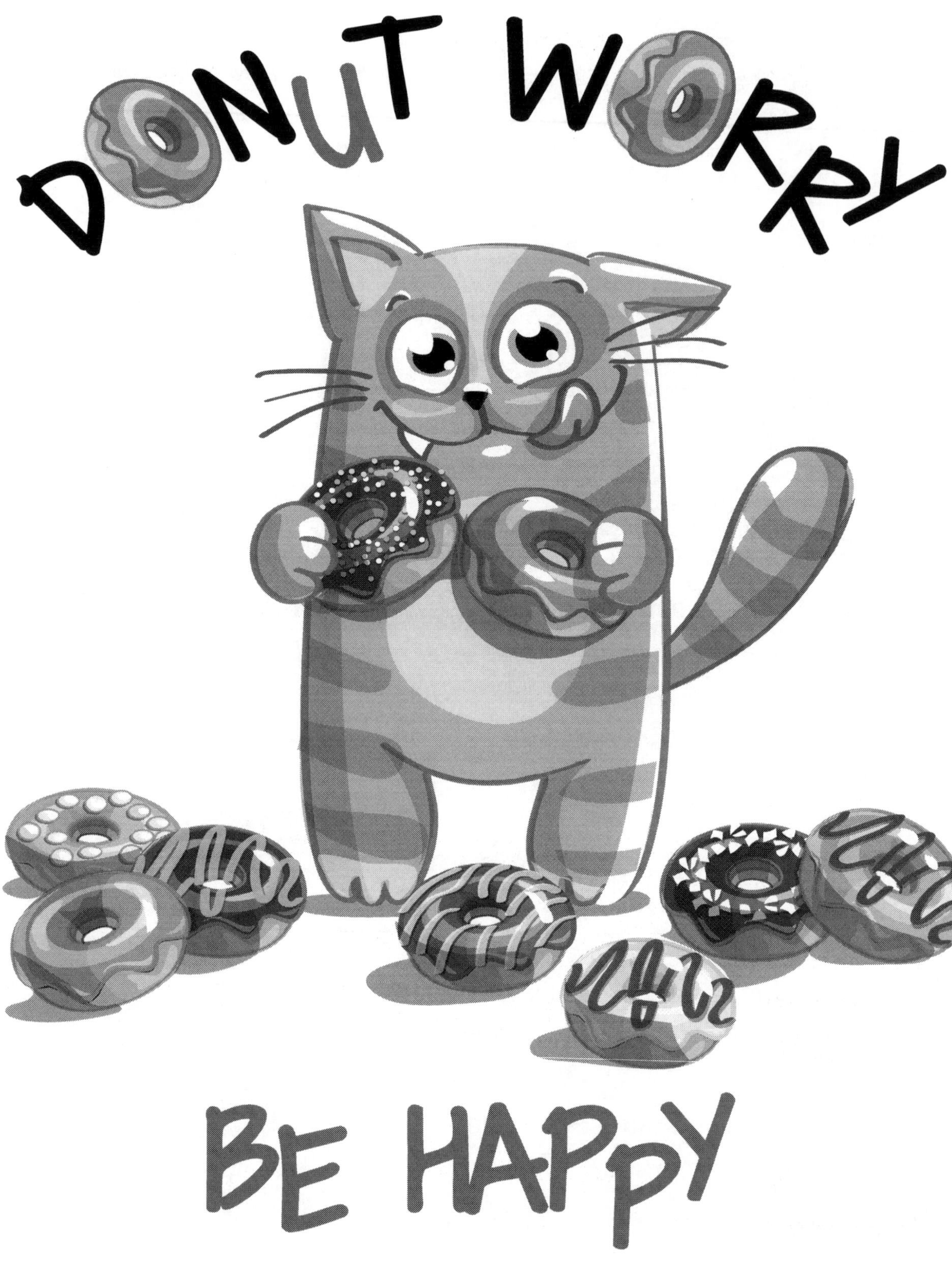
DONUT WORRY
BE HAPPY

# LET'S EAT!

Q. What do you call someone
who studies soda?
A. A FIZZ-iscist.

Q: Why do watermelons have
large family weddings?
A: Because they cantaloupe.

Q: What do you use to
treat a sick lemon?
A: Lemon aid!

Q. Where do you put a
smart hot dog?
A. Honour roll.

Q. How do you make a
sausage roll?
A. Push it.

Q. Why did the sesame spend
the day at the Casino?
A. He was on a roll.

Q. What is worse than finding a
slug in your apple?
A. Finding half a slug in your apple.

49

Q. Why do the French eat snails?
A. They don't like fast food.

Q. What do you call a yam
that's been stolen?
A. A hot potato.

Q. Why was the strawberry so sad?
A. His mother got into a JAM!

Q. What do you call a broken can opener?
A. A can't opener!

Q. What did the baby corn
say to the mommy corn?
A. Where's my pop corn?

Q. Why didn't the orange win the race?
A. It just ran out of juice.

Q. Why did the weight watcher give up
the all almond diet?
A. Because it was just nuts.

Q. Why was the potato such a good detectives?
A. Because he ept his eyes peeled.

Q. Why did the coffee file a police report?
A. It got mugged.

Q. Why did the banana go to the doctor?
A. It just wasn't peeling well.

Q. Did you hear the joke about the cookie?
A. It is crummy.

Q. What did the grape do when
he got stepped on?
A. He let out a little wine.

Q: How do you fix a broken tomato?
A: With tomato paste!

Q. How do you fix a
cracked pumpkin?
A. With a pumpkin
patch.

Q. What do you someone else's cheese?
A. NACHO cheese.

Q: What cheese is made backwards?
A: Edam

Q: What do you get if you cross an apple with a shellfish?
A: A crab apple.

Q. Why did Billy go out with a prune?
A. Because he couldn't find a date!

Q. How does a cucumber become a pickle?
A. It goes through a jarring experience.

Did you hear about the restaurant on the moon?
Great food, no atmosphere.

Q: Why was the cook arrested?
A: Because he was caught beating an egg!

Q: Why don't eggs tell each other jokes?
A: They're aufraid they will crack each other up!

Q. Why wouldn't the boy eat green boogers?
A. He preferred to wait until they were ripe.

Q. What did the vegan use to go hunting?
A. An asparagus spear.

Q. Why was the gherkin so worried?
A. Because he was in a pickle!

Q. Why did the lettuce beat the carrot in a race?
A. Because it was a head!

Q: Where did the lettuce go for a drink?
A: The Salad Bar!

Q. What do you call a fake noodle?
A. An Impasta.

Q. Did you hear about the guy that choked on his ravioli?
A. He pasta way.

Q. Why did the cannibal book a stop over on his holiday?
A. He wanted another leg on his journey.

Two cannibals were eating a clown. One says to the other: "Does this taste funny to you?"

Q. What part of the magician did the cannibal eat first?
A. His incredible feat.

Q What's a cannibal's favourite fruit?
A. Adam's apple.

Q. What do you feed a vegetarian cannibal
A. Ears of corn!

Q. Why did the cannibal go to the gun show?
A. He liked arms.

# UDDERLY FANTASTIC

Q. How do you know when a cow just got out of your bathtub?
A. By the big "C" on his bathrobe.

Q. What do cows read?

A. Cattle-logs.

Q: What do you call a cow on a trampoline?
A: A milk shake!

Q. Where do cows like to go on a date?
A. To the Moovies.

Q. What do you call a cow who plays the piano
A. A moosician.

Q. What do you call a sleeping bull?
A. A bull-dozer.

Q. What did the buffalo say when his son went to off to school?
A. Bison!

Q. Where do cows watch videos?
A. Moo-tube.

Q. What do you call a cow that has no milk?
A. An udder failure.

Q. What do you call cows that do stand up comedy?
A. Laughing stock.

Q. How do cows multiply?
A. With a cowculator.

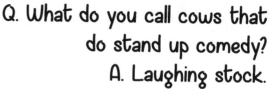

Q. What do you call a two legged cow?
A. Lean beef.

Q. What do you get when you over-indulge a cow?
A. Spoiled milk.

Q. How do you make a cow invisible?
A. Dress it in ca-MOO-flage.

Q. Where did the cows go for their school excursion?
A. To the mooseum.

# WHAT DO YOU CALL THAT?

Q. What do you call a man who can't stand?
A. Neil.

Q. What do you call a man with a car on his head?
A. Jack.

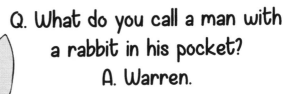

Q. What do you call a man with a rabbit in his pocket?
A. Warren.

Q. What do you call two men standing in the window?
A. Kurt and Rod.

Q. What do you call a pig who knows karate?
A. Pork chop.

Q. What do you call a wizard in space?
A. A flying saucer-er.

Q. What do you call a man with a rubber toe?
A. Robber-toe.

Q. What do you call a girl with a sunlamp on her head?
A. Tanya.

Q. What do you call a dance floor full of snowmen?
A. Snowball.

57

Q. What do you call a man with a piano on his head?
A. An ambulance.

Q. What do you call a man with a spade on his head?
A. Doug.

Q. What do you call a girl with one leg longer than the other?
A. Eileen.

Q. What do you call a multi-story building?
A. A library.

Q. What do you call a man without a spade on his head?
A. Douglas.

Q. What do you call a boomerang that doesn't come back?
A. A stick.

Q. What do you call a horse that likes scrap booking?
A. A hobbyhorse.

# WIT & WEAR

Q. What do lawyers wear
to court?
A. Lawsuits.

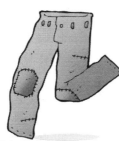

Q. Why was the belt
arrested?
A. Because it was holding
up some pants.

Q. What did the policeman
say to his chest?
A. Freeze. You're under a
vest.

Q. What kind of bow can
never be tied?
A. A rainbow.

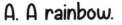

Q. Why did the golfer wear two pairs
of pants?
A. In case he gets a hole in one!

Q. Why do super heroes wear their
Underpants on the outside?
A. To keep their tights up.

Q. What did the hat say to the scarf?
A. You hang around, and I'll go ahead.

Q. Why should you never buy velcro.
A. Because it's a total rip-off.

# WILD WEATHER

Q. What happens if you wear a snowsuit inside?
A. It melts!

Q. Why do the English always take umbrellas
to see the queen?
A. Because she reigns over them.

Q. What colour
is the wind?
A. Blew.

Q. What do clouds
wear under their
trousers?
A. Thunderpants.

Q. What happens
when the fog lifts in
Los Angeles?
A. UCLA.

Q. When does it rain Money?
A. When there is some change in
the weather.

Q. What do you call a
snowman with a sunburn?
A. A puddle.

61

Q. What is a tornadoes' favourite tune?
A. Let's twist again.

Q. How do hurricanes see?
A. With one eye.

Q. Did you hear about the cow that got swept up in a tornado?
A. It was an udder disaster!

Q. What's worse than raining cats and dogs?
A. Hailing taxis!

Q. Why was the lightning bolt arrested?
A. His behaviour was shocking.

Q. What is a bat's favourite type of lightning?
A. Ball lightning!

64

# THE CAT'S MEOW

Q: What did the cat say when the dog stole her food?
A: You've got to be kitten me!

Q. What's a cats favorite colour?
A. Purrrrrple.

Q. What is a cats favourite nursery rhyme?
A. Three blind mice.

Q. Why was the cat arrested?
A. Because he was a purrrpetrator.

Q. What do you call a cat that has no money?
A. A paw-per!

Q. What is it called when a cat wins a beauty contest?
A. A CAT-HAS-TROPHY!

Q. What part of a cat has the most fur?
A: The outside.

Q. What do feral cats carry to survive in the wild?
A. A survival Kit.

Q. Why is it impossible to beat a cat at a video game?
A. Because they have nine lives!

Q. Why do cats like to sit on your keyboard?
A. So they keep their eyes on the mouse.

Q. What looks like half a cat?
A. The other half!

Q. What do you call a cat in a snow storm?
A. A cool cat.

Q. What's the difference between a comma and a cat?
A. One has claws at the end of it's paws, and the other is a pause at the end of a clause.

Q. What do you call a cat wearing lip gloss?
A. Glamourpuss.

Q. How do cat's do their shopping?
A. They order through catalogues.

Q. Why can't leopards ever hide?
A. Because they are always spotted.

Q. What do cats do to keep up with current affairs?
A. The watch the nightly mews.

66

Q. How do cats like their coffee?
A. Purrrrcolated.

Q. What do you call a cat that climbs
mountains?
A. A sher-paw.

Q. What do you get if you
feed a cat vinegar?
A. A sour puss!

Q. What do you call a
cat in a sport scar?
A. A car-pet.

Q. What do you call a cat that
plays the bongos?
A. A Purrrrcussionist.

Q. What do you get if you cross a
cat with Father Christmas?
A. Santa Claws!

Q. What do you call a cat that
works as journalist?
A. A Press Kit.

# KNOCK KNOCK!

Knock knock
Who is there?
Daisy
Some day who?
Some daisys would
look nice in the
garden!

Will you remember
me in 2 minutes?
Yes.
Knock, knock.
Who's there?
Hey, you didn't
remember me!

Knock, knock
Who's there?
Wood shoe
Wood shoe who?
Wood shoe like to
come and play?

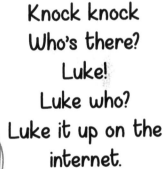

Knock knock
Who's there?
Luke!
Luke who?
Luke it up on the
internet.

Knock knock
Who's there?
Noel
Noel who?
No, there is an L.

Knock knock
Who's there?
Wayne
Wayne who?
Wayne drops keep
falling on my head.

69

Knock knock
Who's there?
Mike!
Mike who?
Mikey won't open the
lock!

Knock! Knock
Who's there?
Dozen.
Dozen who?
Dozen anyone want
to open the door?

Knock! Knock
Who's there?
Witches.
Witches who?
Witches the best
way home?

Knock, knock.
Who's there?
Canoe! Canoe who?
Canoe open the door please?

Knock! Knock
Who's there?
I can't reach the
doorbell!

Knock, Knock
Who's there?
who's there?
Scold.
Scold who?
Open the door,
Scold out here!

Knock knock
Who's there?
Butter
Butter who?
I butter not tell you.

70

Knock, knock
Who's there!
Dewy.
Dewy who?
Do we have to eat
our spinach?

Knock, knock
Who's there?
Broken spear.
Broken spear who?
Oh, forget it, this
joke is utterly
pointless.

Knock knock
Who's There?
Cargo!
Cargo who?
Car go beep, beep!

Knock knock
Who's There?
Who
Who who?
Are you an owl?

Knock, knock
Who's there?
Leaf
Leaf Who?
Don't just leaf me
standing out here!

Knock Knock
Who's there?
Crustacean.
Crustacean who?
We should get off the train
at Kings Crustacean!

71

Knock, knock
Who's there?
Nun
Nun who?
Nun of your business!

Knock knock
Who's there?
Boo
Boo who?
Don't cry, It's only me!

Knock, knock
Who is there?
Teddy!
Teddy who?
Teddy is my birthday!

Knock, knock
Who's there?
An old lady.
An old lady who?
Sorry we don't allow yodelling here!

Knock, knock.
Who's there?
Cash.
Cash who?
No thanks, I prefer peanuts!

Knock! Knock
Who's there?
Radio.
Radio who?
Radio not, here I come!

Knock, knock
Who's there?
Al.
Al who?
If you won't open
the door Al have
to come back
later!

Knock! Knock
Who's there?
From.
From who?
Actually, if you want
to be grammatically
correct you should
say "from whom."

Knock! Knock
Who's there?
Needle.
Needle who?
I Needle all the help
I can get.

Knock knock
Who's there?
Tank!
Tank who?
Don't tank me, I
didn't do anything!

Knock knock
Who's there?  Howard!
Howard who?
Howard you like to go to a
movie?

Knock! Knock
Who's there?
Howl.
Howl who?
Howl I get in if you
don't open the door?

Knock! Knock
Who's there?
Dishes.
Dishes who?
Dishes a nice place
you got here.

Knock knock
Who's there?
Buddha
Buddha who?
I need some Buddha
on my bread!

Knock, knock
Who's there?
Water
Water who?
Water you want?

Knock, knock
Who's there?
Doris.
Doris who?
The Dor-is locked and
I can't get in!

Knock! Knock
Who's there?
Police.
Police who?
Police hurry up and
open the door. It's
freezing out here!

Knock, knock.
Who's there?
Amy.
Amy who?
A-mispalced
my keys!

74

# AFRICA ANIMALS

OOOWWW

FOREST ANIMALS

SEA
ANIMALS

79

# AUSTRALIA ANIMALS

81

# SOUTH AMERICA ANIMALS

PETS

Find the ten differences between the two pictures.

84

**Find the ten differences between the two pictures.**

85

Find the ten differences between the two pictures.

**Find the ten differences between the two pictures.**

87

88

**Find the ten differences between the two pictures.**

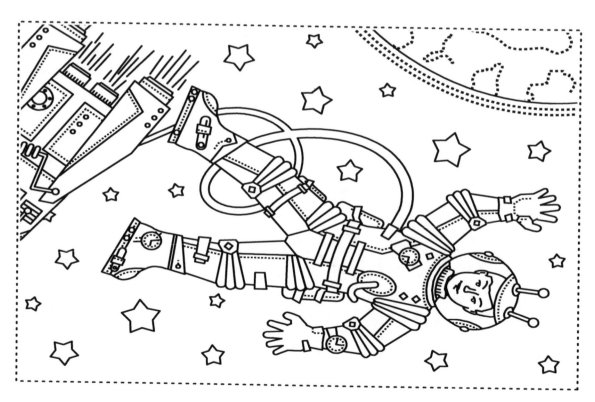

Find the ten differences between the two pictures.

90

**Find the ten differences between the two pictures.**

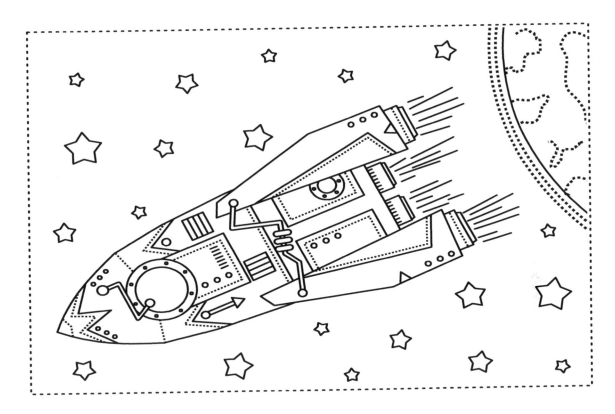

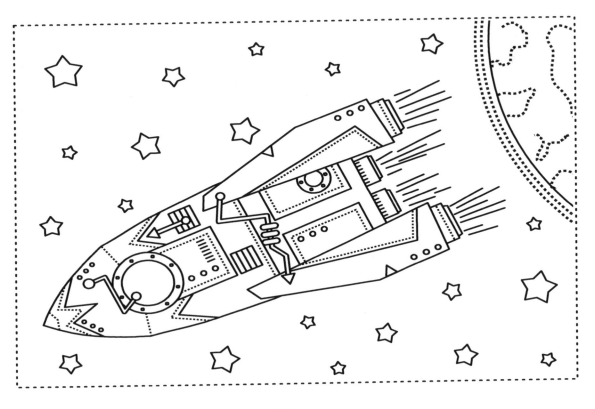

91

Find the ten differences between the two pictures.

92

**Find the ten differences between the two pictures.**

Find the ten differences between the two pictures.

94

**Find the ten differences between the two pictures.**

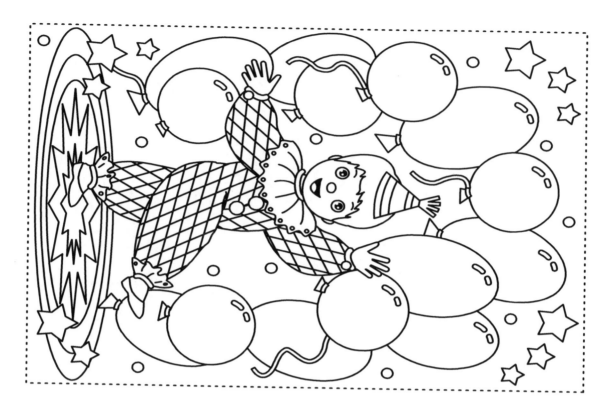

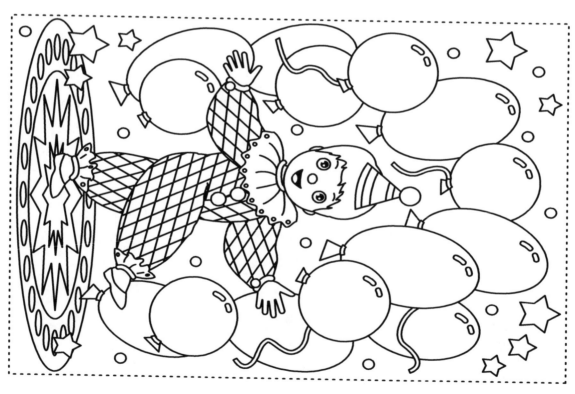

Find the ten differences between the two pictures.

Find the ten differences between the two pictures.

97

Find the ten differences between the two pictures.

98

**Find the ten differences between the two pictures.**

Find the ten differences between the two pictures.

100

86816410R00060

Made in the USA
San Bernardino, CA
30 August 2018